TEAM
PERCUSSION

LORNE PEARCEY &
RICHARD DUCKETT

International Music Publications

Introduction

TEAM PERCUSSION has been designed to meet the needs of young percussionists everywhere, whether lessons are given individually, in groups or in the classroom.

Musical variety

The book contains a wide variety of musical styles, from the Baroque and Classical eras to film, folk, jazz and Latin American. In addition there are original pieces and studies, and technical exercises, progressing from the beginner stage to approximately Grade IV standard of the *Associated Board of the Royal Schools of Music*. Furthermore, TEAM PERCUSSION offers material suitable for mixed percussion ensemble as well as solos with piano accompaniment.

Ensemble pieces

TEAM PERCUSSION contains corresponding pages of music which can be played together in harmony. Beginners are thus given early ensemble experience and the opportunity to share sessions with other players, and occasionally with guitar or keyboard.

The ensemble material in TEAM PERCUSSION integrates with the same material in TEAM BRASS and TEAM WOODWIND, and thus offers exciting possibilities for mixed instrumental lessons, concerts and assemblies.

Study options

TEAM PERCUSSION is not a 'method'. It is a selection of primer material from which the teacher can select a suitably graded course for each pupil. This allows for variation in concentration threshold and tempo of progression. There are also several choices of progressive path the pupil can follow. Study options appear at the foot of appropriate pages. Material for tuned percussion instruments appears on right-hand pages, and material for snare drum and timpani on alternate left-hand pages.

GCSE skills

In addition to fostering musical literacy, Rhythm Grids and Play By Ear lines provide early opportunities for composition and improvisation. This aspect of TEAM PERCUSSION can be a useful starting point for these elements in the GCSE examination course now followed in many secondary schools.

Comprehensive notes on the use of this series, scores of ensemble pieces and piano accompaniments may be found in the ACCOMPANIMENTS book.

Concert pieces

The percussion pieces and piano accompaniments near the end of the book are more suited to concert performance rather than classroom study.

Note:
In some of the earlier pieces in the TEAM PERCUSSION solo book the key signatures appear with bracketed sharps or flats. Whereas each key signature is academically correct, the brackets serve to indicate sharps or flats that have not as yet been introduced to the player. These sharps or flats do not appear in the exercise or piece. On the cue line of the piano accompaniments, however, the key signatures are indicated in the usual way.
Bar numbers have been added to the pieces with piano accompaniments.

Team Percussion Ensemble

TEAM PERCUSSION ensemble material has been specially written so that it can be played by almost any combination of percussion instruments. The pieces almost are basically for tuned percussion duet, to which can be added independent (and inessential) snare drum and timpani parts if required. Other appropriate percussion instruments of indefinite pitch may also be added.

This book contains nine pages of ensemble material. Parts relating to B flat ensemble, which integrate fully with the trumpet and clarinet duets in TEAM BRASS and TEAM WOODWIND, appear on the same numbered pages in all TEAM books. Parts relating to C ensemble material, which may be played as a percussion quartet or together with other C pitched instruments are included in the Supplement. Thus TEAM PERCUSSION may be used on its own, with a small group of brass and/or wind players, or with larger combinations up to full-sized wind orchestra.

TEAM PERCUSSION also contains many other titles which may be played by one or more of the percussion instruments in unison or in harmony with the same titles in TEAM BRASS or TEAM WOODWIND.

All the ensemble material is graded to match the lesson material. The ensemble pieces may easily be located by following the direction at the foot of the appropriate lesson page. Scores for all ensemble material and more extensive notes appear in the ACCOMPANIMENTS book.

The following symbols have been used to provide an immediate visual identification:

     Pieces with piano accompaniment

     Part of an ensemble arrangement
(scores included in ACCOMPANIMENTS book.)

Because the ensemble pieces provide a meeting point for players who are at various stages of development, these may include technical elements (new notes, rhythms, etc.) which are not in fact introduced until some pages later.

Edited by BARRIE CARSON TURNER

Piano accompaniments by BARRIE CARSON TURNER

INTERNATIONAL MUSIC PUBLICATIONS would like to thank the
following publishers for permission to use arrangements
of their copyright material in TEAM PERCUSSION.
BLOWIN' IN THE WIND - Words and Music by BOB DYLAN
© 1963 & 1992 Witmark & Sons, USA
Warner Chappell Music Ltd., London W1Y 3FA
LOVE ME TENDER - Words and Music by VERA MATSON & ELVIS PRESLEY
© 1956 & 1992 Elvis Presley Music Inc., USA
Carlin Music Corp., London NW1 8BD
LITTLE DONKEY - Words and Music by ERIC BOSWELL
© 1959 & 1992 Chappell Music Ltd., London W1Y 3FA
ST LOUIS BLUES - Words and Music by W.C. HANDY
© 1914 & 1992 Handy Brothers Music Co. Inc., USA
Francis, Day & Hunter Ltd., London WC2H 0EA
STAR WARS Main Title - by JOHN WILLIAMS
© 1977 & 1992 Fox Fanfare Music Inc.
Warner Chappell Music Ltd., London W1Y 3FA
BLUE MONK - by THELONIOUS MONK
© 1979 & 1992 Thelonious Music Corporation, USA
Bocu Music Ltd., London W1H 1AR
PEANUT VENDOR - Words by MARION SUNSHINE and L. WOLFE GILBERT
Music by MOISES SIMONS
© 1931 & 1992 E.B. Marks Music Corporation, USA
EMI Music Publishing Ltd., London WC2H 0EA
THE PINK PANTHER - by HENRY MANCINI
© 1963 & 1992 United Artists Music Co., Inc., USA
EMI United Partnership Ltd., London WC2H 0EA
SANDPAPER BALLET - Music by LEROY ANDERSON
© 1992 Mills Music Inc.
Belwin Mills Music Ltd., London WC2H 0EA

Sincere thanks are extended
to the following people whose criticism, advice
and help in various ways has been invaluable.
HUW CEREDIG, Principal Percussionist,
City of Birmingham Symphony Orchestra.
JENNY MARSDEN, Percussionist.
ANNIE OAKLEY, Principal Percussionist,
City of Birmingham, Symphony Orchestra.
And also to the many pupils who have worked with the
TEAM PERCUSSION books in transcript form.

Exclusive Distributors
International Music Publications,
Southend Road, Woodford Green,
Essex IG8 8HN, England.

Cover conception and realisation: Ian Barrett/David Croft
Cover Photography: Ron Goldby
Production: Stephen Clark/David Croft
Props: Meynell Paints Ltd.
Reprographics: Highlight Reprographics
Instruments photographed by courtesy of Percussion Plus and Redbridge Music School
Typeset by: Headline Publicity Ltd.
Music setting by Gillian Gower/Christine Mitchell
Printed in England by Halstan & Co. Ltd.

TEAM PERCUSSION
ISBN 0 86359 863 3 / Order Ref: 17791 / 215-2-716

Lesson diary & practice chart

Date (week commencing)	Enter number of minutes practised.							Teacher indicates which pages to study.
	Mon	Tue	Wed	Thur	Fri	Sat	Sun	

The Instruments

Snare Drum

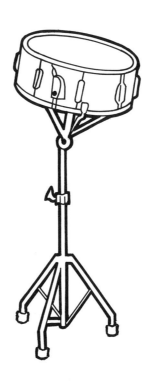

Timpani

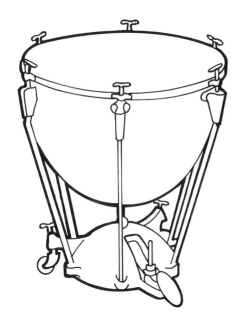

Pedal Timpani

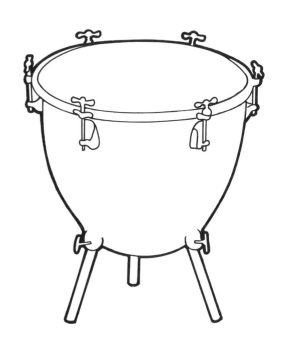

Hand Timpani

Tuned Percussion

Glockenspiel

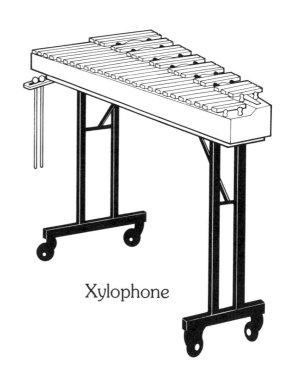

Xylophone

Sticks and Mallets

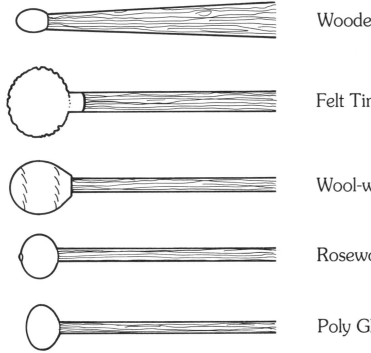

Wooden Drum Stick

Felt Timpani Mallet

Wool-wound Vibes/Marimba Mallet

Rosewood Xylophone Mallet

Poly Glockenspiel Mallet

*French time names may be used

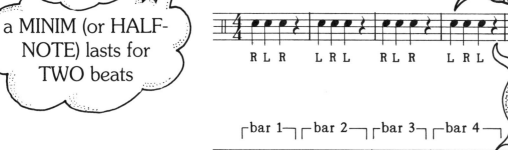

The TIME SIGNATURE 4/4 means each bar must add up to FOUR beats

a MINIM (or HALF-NOTE) lasts for TWO beats

A CROTCHET (or QUARTER-NOTE) lasts for ONE beat

A CROTCHET REST lasts for ONE beat

PULSE - clap or beat time

■ This page may be played with TEAM BRASS and/or TEAM WOODWIND.

Start with G...

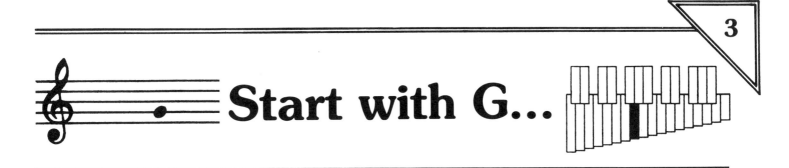

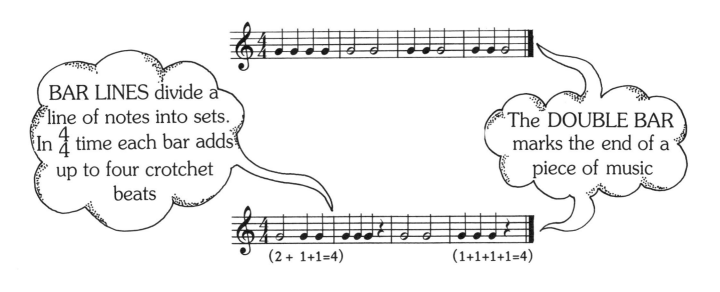

BAR LINES divide a line of notes into sets. In $\frac{4}{4}$ time each bar adds up to four crotchet beats

The **DOUBLE BAR** marks the end of a piece of music

(2 + 1+1=4)   (1+1+1+1=4)

...then on to A

A's and G's

Pavane

Slowly and sadly

■ Proceed to B on page 5; or F on page 7.

Start with G...

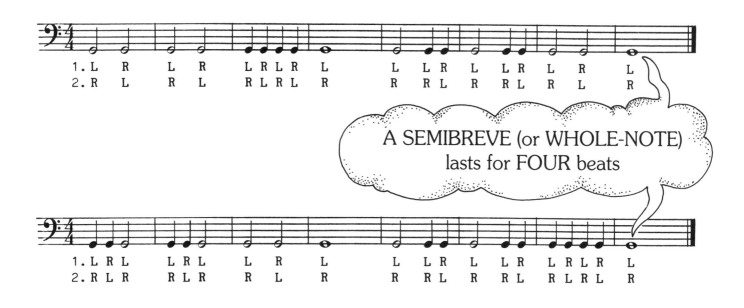

A SEMIBREVE (or WHOLE-NOTE) lasts for FOUR beats

... then on to D

Sort 'em out!

This piece can be played in conjunction with *Sort e'm out!* opposite.

March tempo

9

■ Proceed to Damping on page 8; Low F & B♭ on page 12.

The note B

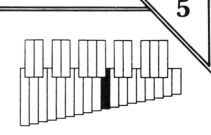

Au clair de la lune

Traditional

Tricky tune!

The note C

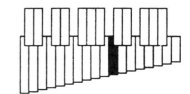

Flowing

Two bar phrase (1) | Two bar phrase (2) | Two bar phrase (3) | Two bar phrase (4)

Sort 'em out!

This piece can be played in conjunction with *Sort e'm out!* opposite.

March tempo

Single and Double Strokes

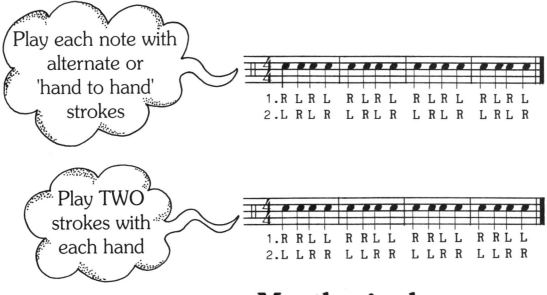

Play each note with alternate or 'hand to hand' strokes

1. R L R L R L R L R L R L R L R L
2. L R L R L R L R L R L R L R L R

Play TWO strokes with each hand

1. R R L L R R L L R R L L R R L L
2. L L R R L L R R L L R R L L R R

Mostly singles

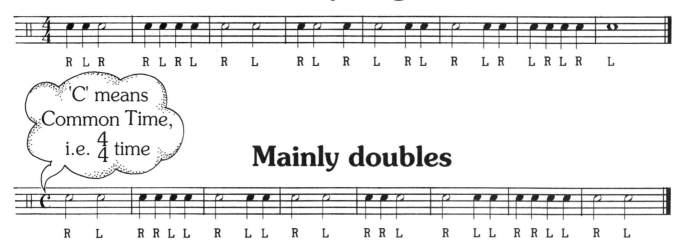

R L R R L R L R L R L R L R L R L R L R L R L R L

'C' means Common Time, i.e. $\frac{4}{4}$ time

Mainly doubles

R L R R L L R L L R L R R L R L L R R L L R L

Acapulco Bay

This piece can be played in conjunction with *Acapulco Bay* opposite.
Tambourine part for *Acapulco Bay* is located in the SUPPLEMENT.

Tempo di beguine

R R L L R L R L R L R L R L R L R R L L R

9

R L R R L R L L R L R L R R L R R L R L R L

■ Proceed to Paradiddles on page 10; Quavers on page 16; related ensemble material on pages 14 & 15.

The note F

Acapulco Bay

This piece can be played in conjunction with *Acapulco Bay* below.

Tempo di beguine

The note B♭

The FLAT lowers the pitch of a note by one semitone

Ode to joy

LUDWIG VAN BEETHOVEN
(1770-1827)

Acapulco Bay

This piece can be played in conjunction with *Acapulco Bay* above.

Tempo di beguine

■ For related ensemble material see SUPPLEMENT pages 14 & 15 (upper parts of duets).

Damping

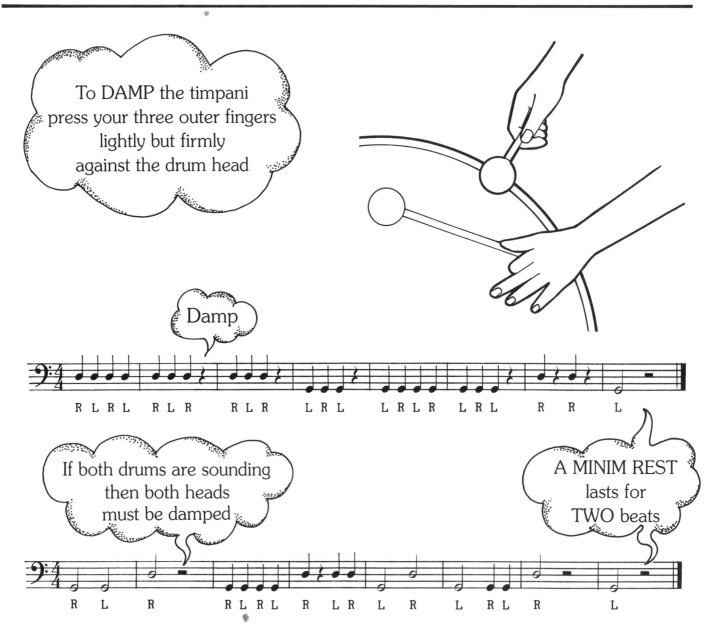

Mind the gap!

■ Proceed to Low F & B♭ on page 12.

The key signature of F major

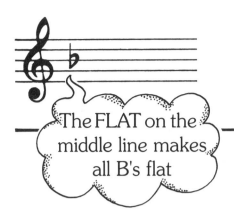

Little robin redbreast

Traditional

Step round

Welsh tune

Traditional

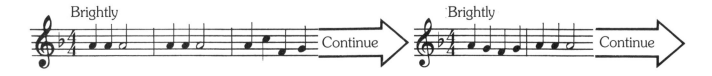

Single Paradiddles

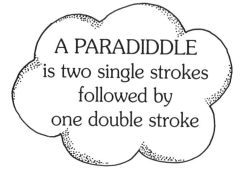

A PARADIDDLE
is two single strokes
followed by
one double stroke

1. R L R R L R L L R L R R L R L L
2. L R L L R L R R L R L L R L R R

R L R L R R L R L R L R L R L R R L L R L R R L

R L R L R L R L R R L R L L R L R L R L R L L R

Steady beat

Duet

3/4 time

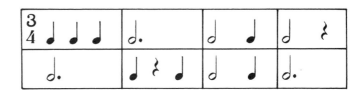

Slow waltz

Composed by eleven-year old JOANNE AHMED

Every bar adds up to three crotchets

Four bar question phrase, A — Four bar answer phrase, B

A DOTTED MINIM lasts for THREE beats

This means 'rest' for 4 whole bars - so count ① 2 3 ② 2 3 ③ 2 3 ④ 2 3 and then play from bar 5

Les ballons

Triangle part for *Les Ballons* is located in the SUPPLEMENT.

Gently and dreamily

getting slower

Round lullaby

The notes
Low F & B♭

Two rounds

Li'l Liza Jane

■ For related ensemble material see pages 14 & 15; C on page 18; Quavers on page 18.

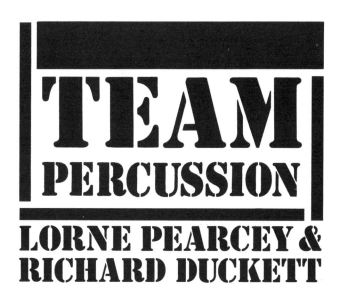

Supplement

International Music Publications

Tambourine

The Tambourine may be played
in conjunction with *Acapulco Bay*.

Acapulco Bay

(Tambourine part)

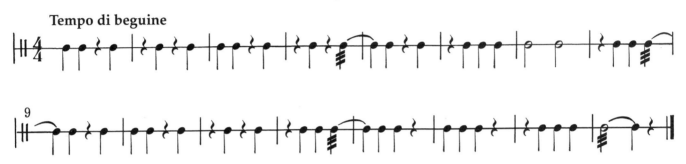

11

Triangle

The Triangle may be played in
conjunction with *Les ballons*.

Les ballons

(Triangle part)

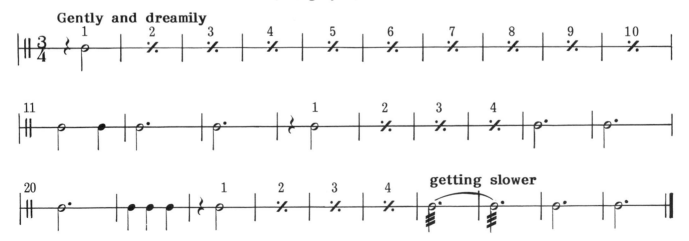

German tune
(Timpani part with tuned percussion/flute/oboe duet)

Traditional

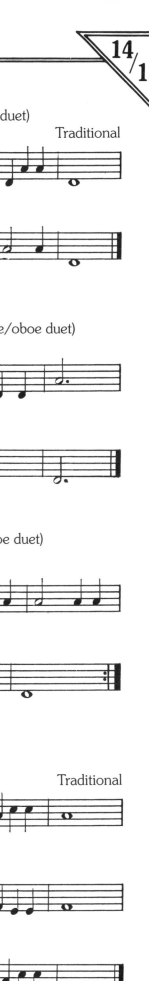

Lullaby
(Timpani part with tuned percussion/flute/oboe duet)

COUNT: ① 2 3 ② 2 3 *soft*

Canzonetta
(Timpani part with tuned percussion/flute/oboe duet)

Fast

A

loud

German tune
(Tuned percussion duet; Timpani part above)

Traditional

14

Lullaby
(Tuned percussion duet; for Timpani part see Supplement page 3)

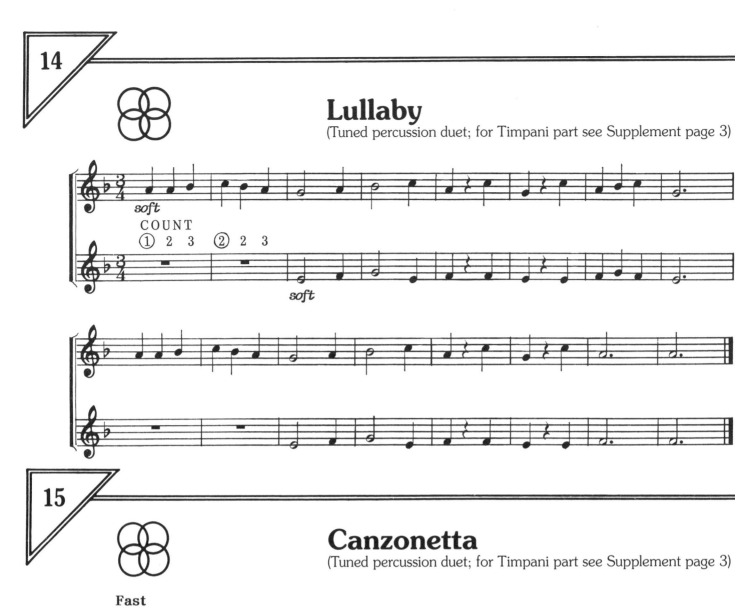

soft

COUNT ① 2 3 ② 2 3

soft

15

Canzonetta
(Tuned percussion duet; for Timpani part see Supplement page 3)

Fast
(Polyphonic texture)

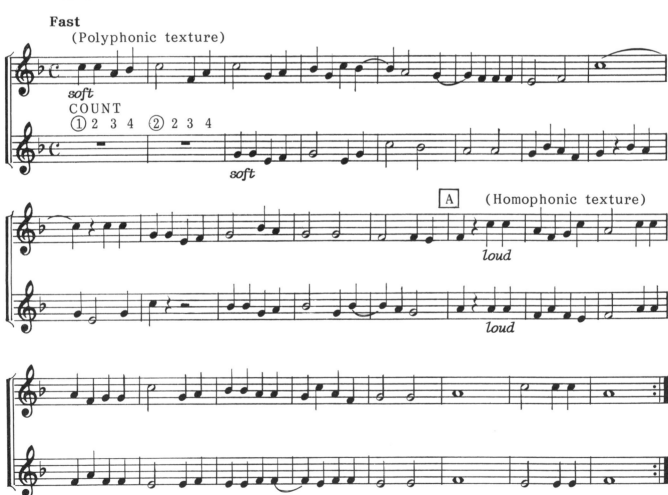

soft

COUNT ① 2 3 4 ② 2 3 4

soft

A (Homophonic texture)

loud

loud

Blowin' in the wind

(Timpani part with B♭ trumpet/clarinet duet)

Words and Music by
BOB DYLAN

Blowin' in the wind

(Timpani part with tuned percussion/flute/oboe duet)

Words and Music by
BOB DYLAN

Blowin' in the wind

(Tuned percussion duet; for Timpani part see opposite)

Words and Music by
BOB DYLAN

Accompaniment
for keyboard on
samba rhythm
setting

Play three times, then on to chorus

4/4	C	F	G	C	C	F	G	G7

Chorus

F	G	C	Am	F	G	C	C

22

Rickshaws
(Woodblock part)

37

Au clair de la lune
(Timpani part)

Traditional

Little donkey
(Temple Blocks part)

Words and Music by
ERIC BOSWELL

Little donkey
(Timpani part)

Words and Music by
ERIC BOSWELL

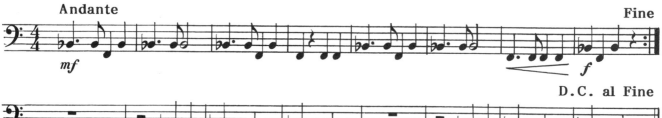

Tijuana brass
(Timpani part)

Brightly

f

I saw three ships
(Timpani part)

Traditional

Happily

mf

Michael row the boat ashore
(Tuned percussion duet)

Moderately

Traditional

mp

mp

Canzona
Part 1

ADRIANO BANCHIERI
(1568-1634)

Canzona
Part 2

ADRIANO BANCHIERI
(1568-1634)

O little town of Bethlehem

(Timpani part)

Traditional

St. Anthony Chorale

(Timpani part)

JOSEPH HAYDN
(1732-1809)

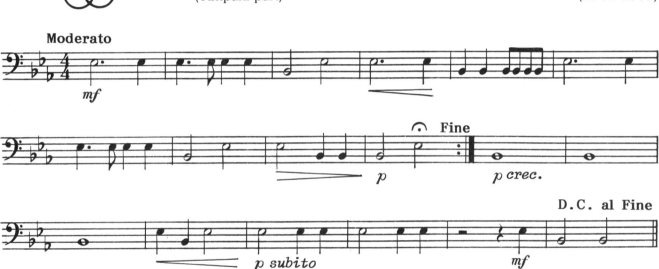

March

from *Judas Maccabaeus*
(Timpani part)

GEORGE FRIDERIC HANDEL
(1685-1759)

The note Upper D

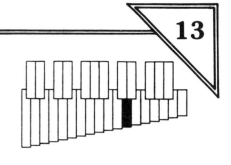

Twinkle, twinkle, little star

Round

Traditional

(1)   (2)

The note E

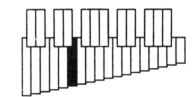

One man and his dog

Traditional

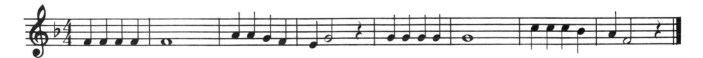

■ For related ensemble material see pages 14 & 15; Quavers on page 17.

German tune
(Snare drum part with all ensemble arrangements)

Traditional

German tune
(Timpani part with B♭ trumpet/clarinet duet)

Traditional

Lullaby
(Timpani part with B♭ trumpet/clarinet duet)

WHOLE - BAR REST
(in any time signature)

COUNT
① 2 3 ② 2 3   soft

Canzonetta
(Timpani part with B♭ trumpet/clarinet duet)

Fast   13   A

loud

■ Ensemble material for C pitched instruments is located in the SUPPLEMENT.

Tied notes

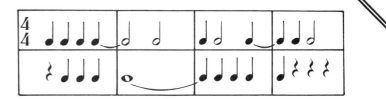

A minim tied to a crotchet lasts for 3 beats

A crotched tied to a crotchet lasts for 2 beats.

A semibreve tied to a crotchet lasts for 5 beats, and so on.

German tune
(Tuned Percussion descant with B♭ trumpet/clarinet duet)

Traditional

Lullaby
(Tuned Percussion descant with B♭ trumpet/clarinet duet)

COUNT
① 2 3 ② 2 3

soft

Canzonetta
(Tuned Percussion descant with B♭ trumpet/clarinet duet)

Fast
(Polyphonic texture)

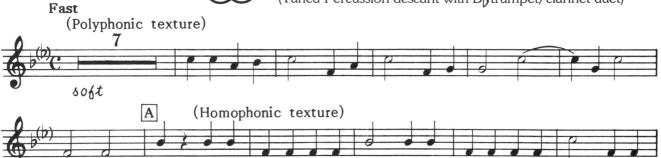

soft

A (Homophonic texture)

loud

■ Ensemble material for C pitched instruments is located in the SUPPLEMENT.

Back around

Here we go!

Words and Music by
eleven-year old JOANNE O'NEILL

1

Phrase A

Here we go, run-ning in the snow,

2

Phrase B

Hav-ing lots of fun now the win-ter's just begun.

3

Phrase A repeated (same word rhythms)

Once a year comes the festive cheer:

4

Phrase C

Mer - ry Christmas and Hap-py New Year!

Single-Stroke Roll

1. R L R L R L R L
2. L R L R L R L R

Single Paradiddle

1. R L R R L R L L
2. L R L L R L R R

■ For related ensemble material see page 20 & 21; Dotted Crotchets on page 22; Quavers in $\frac{6}{8}$ time on page 34.

Quavers

Roundabout

Sleigh Bells

The Sleigh Bells may be played in conjunction with *Sleigh ride.*

Sleigh ride

■ Quavers in $\frac{6}{8}$ time on page 35.

The note C

Skip to my Lou

Traditional

Steady

When the saints go marching in

Traditional

Bouncy

The WHOLE-BAR rest is also a SEMIBREVE rest

■ For related ensemble material see pages 20 & 21; Dotted Crotchets on page 24.

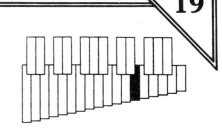

Upper E

Pattern

Phrase A | Phrase B | Phrase A repeated | Phrase C

Morning

EDVARD GRIEG
(1843-1907)

Upper F

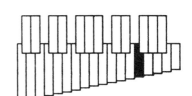

Amazing grace

The QUAVER TRIPLET means that three quavers are played in the time of one crotchet

Traditional

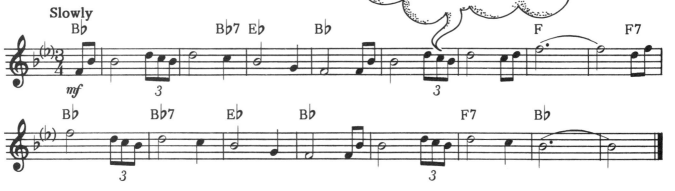

play by ear

Fast and jolly — Continue

Jazzily — Continue

■ For related ensemble material see pages 20 & 21; Upper G on page 23.

Regal fanfare

(Snare Drum part with all ensemble arrangements)

Regal fanfare

(Timpani part with B♭ trumpet/clarinet duet)

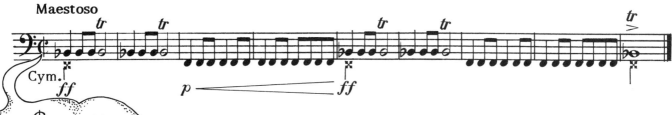

> ₵ means
> TWO MINIM BEATS
> in each bar,
> i.e. $\frac{2}{2}$ time
> (Sometimes called
> ALLA BREVE time).

When I first came to this land

(Snare Drum part with all ensemble arrangements)

Traditional

When I first came to this land

(Timpani part with B♭ trumpet/clarinet duet)

Traditional

■ Ensemble material for C pitched instruments is located in the SUPPLEMENT.

On the repeat, omit these bars and go straight to the bar marked 2

Blowin' in the wind
(Tuned Percussion descant with B♭ trumpet/clarinet duet)

Words and Music
by BOB DYLAN

Accompaniment for keyboard on samba rhythm setting

Play three times, then on to chorus

B♭ version	4	B♭	E♭	F	B♭	B♭	E♭	F	F7
C version	4	C	F	G	C	C	F	G	G7

Chorus

E♭	F	B♭	Gm	E♭	F	B♭	B♭
F	G	C	Am	F	G	C	C

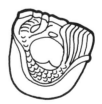

Woodblock

Two-Tone Woodblock

Temple Blocks

The Woodblock may be played in conjunction with *Rickshaws* on page 22.

The Temple Blocks may be played in conjunction with *Little donkey* on page 37.

■ Ensemble material for C pitched instruments is located in the SUPPLEMENT.

Dotted crotchets

Join the dots to make the dotted-crotchet/ quaver effect

Rickshaws

Quite fast

f

Fine

p

D.C. al Fine

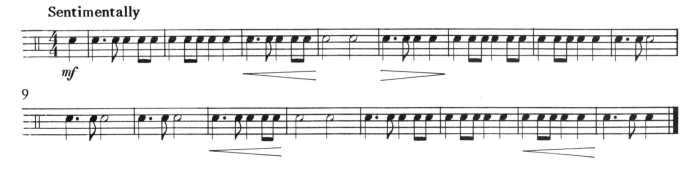

This stands for DA CAPO AL FINE, which means go back to the beginning and finish at the bar marked FINE

Auld lang syne Scottish traditional

This piece can be played in conjunction with *Auld lang syne* opposite.

Sentimentally

mf

9

■ Proceed to Semiquavers on page 26.

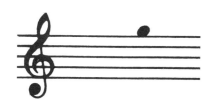

Upper G

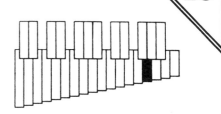

Join the dots to make the dotted-crotchet/quaver effect

New World Symphony

ANTONIN DVOŘÁK
(1841-1904)

Quick march

Composed by nine-year old
REBECKA ELEY

Auld lang syne

Scottish traditional

This piece can be played in conjunction with *Auld lang syne* opposite.

■ Proceed to F# & Upper A on page 25.

Dotted crotchets in

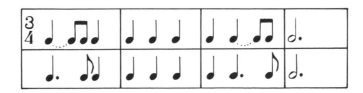

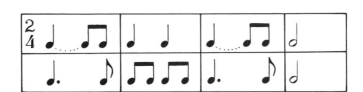

Scottish ballad

D.S. al Fine stands for DAL SEGNO, which means go back to the sign (bar 3), and finish at the bar marked FINE

■ Proceed to Semiquavers on page 28.

The notes F♯ & Upper F♯

The SHARP raises the pitch of a note by one semitone

Workin' on the railroad

Traditional

Like a jolly cowboy saloon song

Coventry carol

Traditional

Moderato

The NATURAL sign cancels the effect of the sharp or flat

Upper A

The small line above the stave is called a LEGER LINE

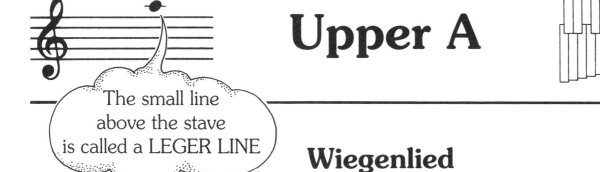

Wiegenlied

Traditional

Happily

slowing down   back to first speed

■ Proceed to Semiquavers on page 27; E♭ on page 29.

Semiquavers

Semiquavers are also called
SIXTEENTH-NOTES

Double-Stroke Roll

1. R R L L R R L L R R L L R R L L
2. L L R R L L R R L L R R L L R R

Step three

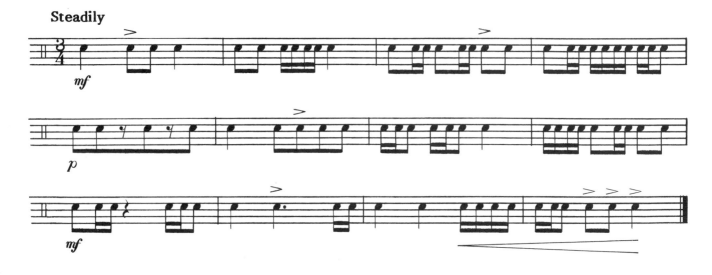

■ Proceed to Dotted Quavers on page 30.

Upper C#

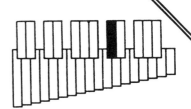

Semiquaver study

Sticking to the point

Moderato

Sticking to the beat

Allegro vivo

■ Proceed to Dotted Quavers on page 32.

The notes E♭ & Upper E♭

Morning has broken

 Traditional

The key signature of B♭ major

Waltz

from *The Sleeping Beauty*

PETER ILYICH TCHAIKOVSKY
(1840-1893)

Dotted quavers

John Brown's body

Traditional

Marziale

mf

f

Improvise

■ 6/8 time on page 34.

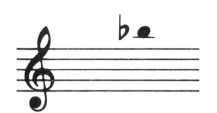

Upper B♭

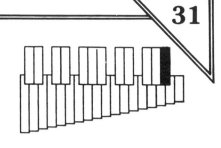

Canon

GUSTAV MAHLER
(1860-1911)

Joy to the world

GEORGE FRIDERIC HANDEL
(1685-1759)

Say 'goodbye'
from *The Marriage of Figaro*

WOLFGANG AMADEUS MOZART
(1756-1791)

■ For related ensemble material see page 37.

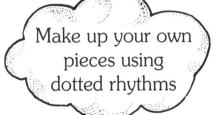

Make up your own pieces using dotted rhythms

La Réjouissance

from *Music for the Royal Fireworks*

GEORGE FRIDERIC HANDEL
(1685-1759)

■ 6/8 time on page 36; E♭ on page 36.

Upper B

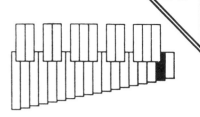

The key signature of D major

Polovtsian dance

ALEXANDER BORODIN
(1833-1887)

Lilting, not fast

mp(mf)

Upper C

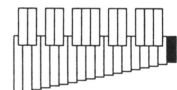

Yankee Doodle

Traditional

Sprightly

mf

Love me tender

Words and Music by
VERA MATSON &
ELVIS PRESLEY

Caressingly

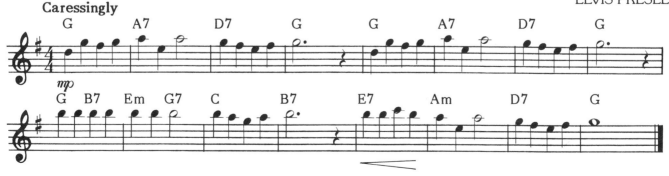

mp

■ 6/8 time on page 35.

6/8 time

and its relationship with 2/4 time.

Orchestral Cymbals

Concert Bass Drum

The Orchestral Cymbals and Concert Bass Drum
may be played in conjunction with *Liberty Bell*.

Liberty Bell

JOHN PHILIP SOUSA
(1854-1932)

When Johnny comes marching home

Traditional

Celtic lullaby

play by ear

■ For related ensemble material see page 39; Quaver Syncopation on page 41; G♯ / A♭ on page 41.

The note E♭

Not too fast

The centipede's masterpiece

Composed by fifteen-year old
SARAH HART

Jolly

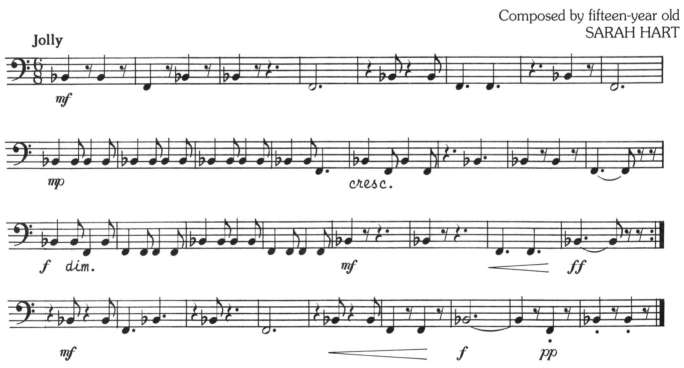

■ For related ensemble material see page 39; Quaver Syncopation on page 40; A & E on page 40.

Au clair de la lune

Traditional

The sharp, flat or natural sign
is called an ACCIDENTAL.
The sign affects all the following notes of the
SAME PITCH WITHIN THAT BAR,
e.g. both B's in this bar are natural, not just the first one

Little donkey

Words and Music by
ERIC BOSWELL

■ Ensemble parts for Timpani and Temple Blocks are located in the SUPPLEMENT.

Flams

Flam

1.	L R	L	R	L	R	L	R
2.	R L	R	L	R	L	R	L
3.	L R	R	L	L	R	R	L
4.	R L	L	R	R	L	L	R

Flam time
Duet

Flam Tap

1.	L R	R	R L	L	L
2.	R L	L	L R	R	R

Flam Accent

L R L R R L R L

■ Proceed to Drags on page 42.

Ensemble parts for Timpani are located in the SUPPLEMENT.

The notes A & E

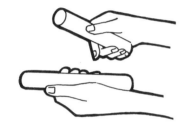

Claves

3-2 Clave rhythm:

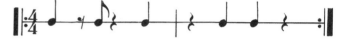

2-3 Clave rhythm:
(or Reverse Clave)

The Claves may be played in conjunction with *Caribbean Dance*, below.

Caribbean dance

Traditional

■ Proceed to Rolls on page 44.

West Indian carnival

The notes G♯ & A♭

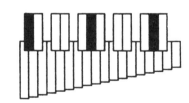

The key signature of A major

Canon

THOMAS TALLIS
(1505-1585)

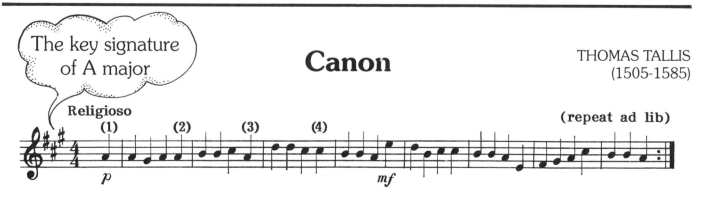

Drags

Drag

Single Drag Tap

Dragoon

St. Louis Blues

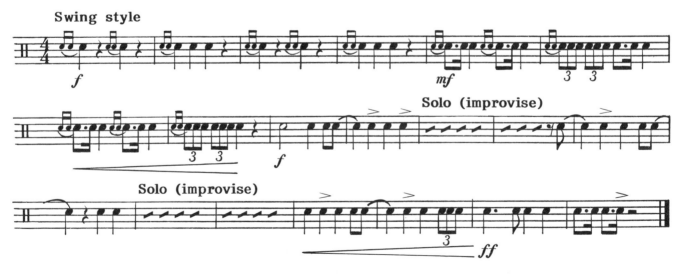

■ Proceed to 5 Stroke Rolls on page 46.

Low D

Three blind mice

Traditional

Middle C
& Low C♯

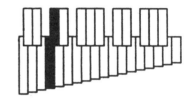

Try ROLLING the longer notes to give them their full value

The entertainer

SCOTT JOPLIN
(1868-1917)

Rolls

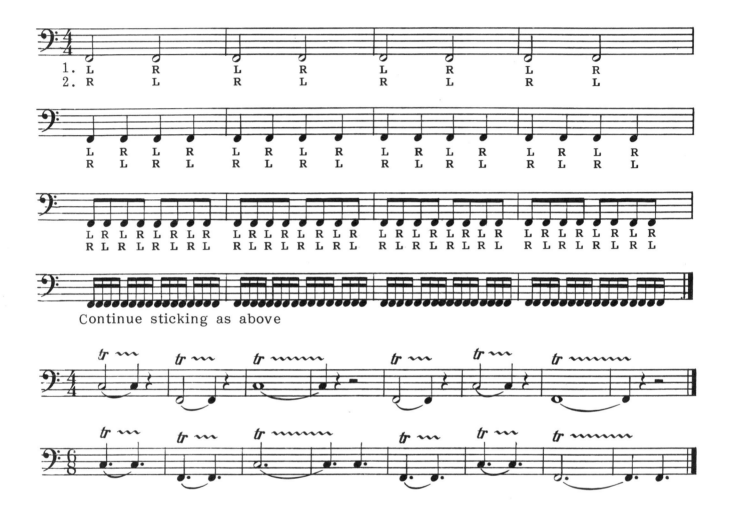

Continue sticking as above

Roll away

■ For related ensemble material see page 48 & 49; Crossing Over/Double Strokes on page 50.

Star Wars main theme

JOHN WILLIAMS

D.S. al ⊕ Coda means
repeat the section
from •𝄋• to ⊕
and then cut to
the CODA section

The swinger

Twelve bar Blues

Accompaniment for keyboard
on '16 beat' rhythm setting

$\frac{4}{4}$	: E♭m	E♭m	E♭m	E♭m	A♭m	A♭m
	E♭m	E♭m	B♭7	A♭m	E♭m	E♭m :|

5-Stroke Rolls

1. RRLL R   RRLL R   RRLL R   RRLL R
2. LLRR L   LLRR L   LLRR L   LLRR L
3. RRLL R   LLRR L   RRLL R   LLRR L

Rhythm and roll

■ Longer rolls on page 52.

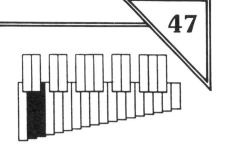

Low B & Low A

Greensleeves

Traditional

Low B♭

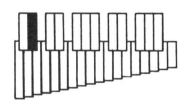

Fossils
from *Carnival of the Animals*

CAMILLE SAINT-SAËNS
(1835-1922)

■ For related ensemble material see page 48 & 49; Low G on page 51.

Michael row the boat ashore

(Timpani part for two drums)

Moderately Traditional

Michael row the boat ashore

(Timpani part for three drums)

Moderately Traditional

Canzona

(Part for Tambour or Snare Drum without snares)

ADRIANO BANCHIERI
(1568-1634)

Allegro

Canzona

(Timpani part for three drums)

ADRIANO BANCHIERI
(1568-1634)

Allegro

■ Parts for Tuned Percussion duet are located in the SUPPLEMENT.

O little town of Bethlehem

Moderato

Traditional

St. Anthony Chorale

JOSEPH HAYDN
(1732-1809)

Moderato

Fine

D.C. al Fine

■ Parts for Timpani are located in the SUPPLEMENT.

Solo for two timpani

■ Proceed to Triplet Rhythms on page 54.

Low G

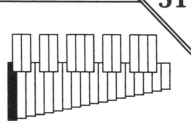

L.A. Nitespot
Twelve bar Blues

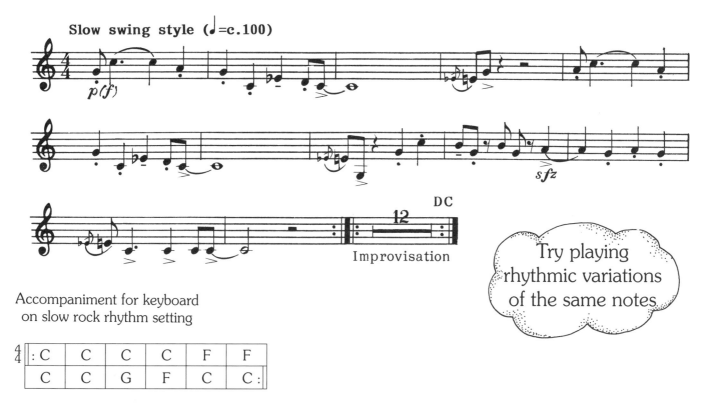

Try playing rhythmic variations of the same notes

Improvisation

Accompaniment for keyboard
on slow rock rhythm setting

$\frac{4}{4}$: C	C	C	C	F	F
C	C	G	F	C	C :

Pomp and Circumstance March No.4

EDWARD ELGAR
(1857-1934)

Longer Rolls

9-Stroke Roll   17-Stroke Roll

1. RRLLRRLL R   1. RRLLRRLLRRLLRRLL R   1. RRLLRRLLRRLLRRLLRRLLRRLLRRLLRRLL
2. LLRRLLRR L   2. LLRRLLRRLLRRLLRR L   2. LLRRLLRRLLRRLLRRLLRRLLRRLLRRLLRR

Overture
from *The Thieving Magpie*

GIOACCHINO ANTONIO ROSSINI
(1792-1868)

Chromatics

Dance of the Sugar-Plum Fairy
from *The Nutcracker*

PETER ILYICH TCHAIKOVSKY
(1840-1893)

Blue Monk
Duet

THELONIUS MONK
(1920-1982)

High F

Triplet trouble

Intervals

C Chromatic scale

March
from Judas Maccabaeus

GEORGE FRIDERIC HANDEL
(1685-1759)

The peanut vendor

Music and Spanish words by
MOISES SIMONS

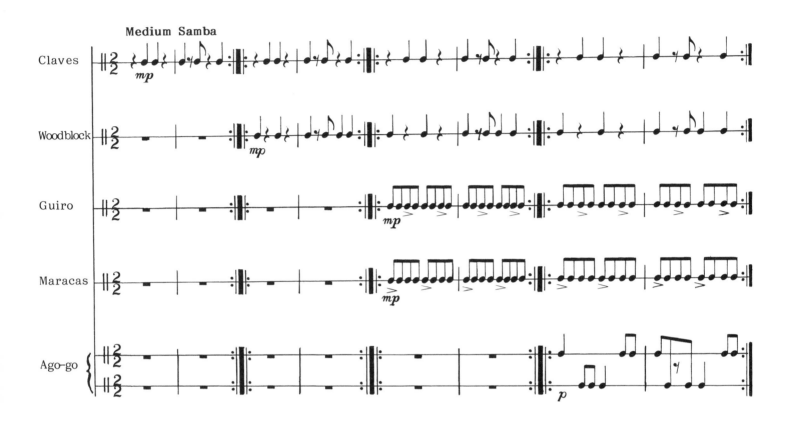

Symphony No.5
(Movement IV)

LUDWIG VAN BEETHOVEN
(1770-1827)

España

EMMANUEL CHABRIER
(1841-1894)

The Pink Panther

HENRY MANCINI

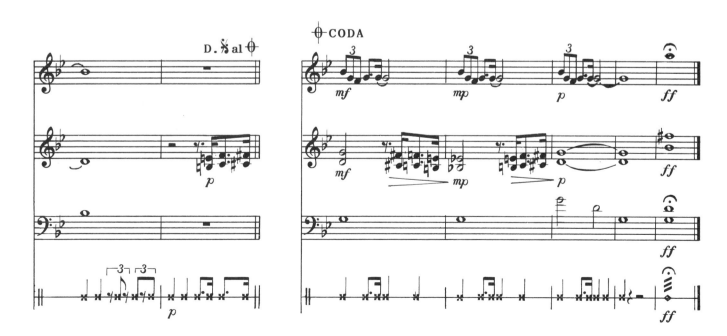

Sandpaper ballet

LEROY ANDERSON

Sandpapers: A (Fine, on blocks) - B (Coarse, on blocks) - C (Coarse, one block with one sheet laid on snare drum.)